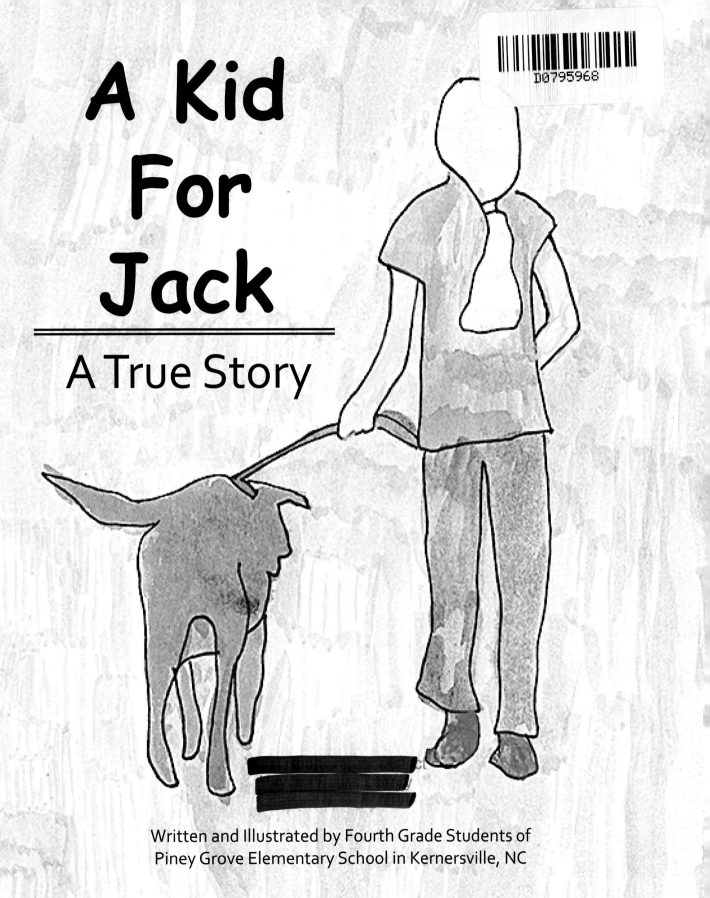

A Kid
For
Jack

A True Story

Written and Illustrated by Fourth Grade Students of
Piney Grove Elementary School in Kernersville, NC

Scholastic Inc.   New York   Toronto   London   Auckland   Sydney   Mexico City   New Delhi   Hong Kong   Buenos Aires

ORIGINAL COVER

Jack did not have a collar because Jack

did not have a home. He was a stray dog

who ate food from garbage cans and slept in

piles of leaves.

But Jack wanted a real home and he wanted

a kid. Not just any kid. A kid who would

scratch his belly, fill his dishes and play fetch

with him.

All alone, Jack wandered into the middle

of the road.

Whoosh.

Thump.

Jack was hit. He tried to hobble to the side

of the road but the pain stopped him.

e blinked slowly, again and again. When he opened his eyes, he saw a woman coming toward him.

"You poor dog," the woman said. Maybe she would give Jack a real home and a kid of his own.

Jack tried to wag his tail. He closed his eyes instead. Everything went black.

When he woke up, his back leg hurt.

He couldn't get up. A man in a white

coat stroked Jack's head.

"Rest, big guy," the vet whispered. "We need

to operate on your hip. Then you will be as

good as new." Maybe this would be Jack's real

home.

The medicine made Jack fall asleep. He

dreamed of finding a kid of his own.

The next day, Jack was not as good as new. He could not stand. He needed medicine for pain and keeping infections away. He needed to stay with the friendly people at the veterinary hospital until he could walk.

When he felt better, Jack was loaded into a car and taken to the Forsyth Correctional Center. Maybe this would be Jack's real home.

There were no kids, but there was a big grassy field and other dogs. He was given his own crate. A man rubbed Jack's belly.

"Welcome to the New Leash on Life Program, Jack," the head trainer greeted him.

ack was scared. That night he went to

sleep scared, he woke up scared, and he

was taken out to the field scared.

Then Jack met his trainer - an inmate at the prison. It was like all the scared flew out of him. The trainer gave Jack treats and scratched his belly when he learned something new. Jack made four new dog friends at the program. He learned to sit, stay, heel and lie down.

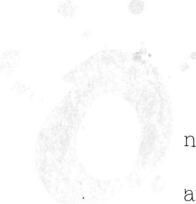n the day of graduation, Jack got an unpleasant surprise. He was not allowed to graduate because his hip was still healing. New dogs entered the program and Jack could show off. He was proud because he knew more than any of the other dogs.

After another four weeks, it was time to find Jack a real home. Volunteers from the Humane Society brought poodles, cute puppies, Chihuahuas, and schnauzers to the Honey Bee Festival in town hoping to find loving families to adopt them. And they brought Jack, too. Maybe Jack would find a real home.

The children loved the energetic puppies. But Jack was a big, one-year-old dog (that's seven in dog years) who walked with a limp. He had to wait for kids to notice him. He was about to give up hope when a boy and a girl came over to him. They smelled like cotton candy and gave loving hugs. A reporter took a picture of Jack and his new friends

That night Jack went to sleep happy, he woke up happy, and he trained with his trainer happy.

A few days later, the girl came to the prison. Her name was Lily and she brought her older sister, little brother, parents and her dog. They all played in the grassy field.

"It looks like Jack likes us," Lily's dad said.

ack had to say goodbye to his trainer.

"You be a good boy now, Jack." His

trainer gave him a final treat.

hen Jack hopped into the minivan.

He went to his real home.

Jack got more than he wanted. He had

three kids to scratch his belly, fill his dish and

play fetch with him. And the three kids got a

lifetime of doggy kisses.

 **T**his is Jack. He lives in Kernersville,

North Carolina. He loves running, dinner

time and belly rubs.

Meet the Authors

Sydney Taylor, Samantha Reagan, Nicole Hamm, Cora McAnulty,

Corbin Lanowitz, Ethan Gilkey, Hannah Martin, Kevin Holland,

Nadia Lischke, Henry Blake, Katie Brinckerhoff,

and Maggie Bryson in front

Kids Are Authors®
Books written by children for children

The Kids Are Authors® Competition was established in 1986 to encourage
children to read and to become involved in the creative process of writing.
Since then, thousands of children have written and illustrated books as participants
in the Kids Are Authors® Competition.

The winning books in the annual competition are published by Scholastic Inc.
and are distributed by Scholastic Book Fairs throughout the United States.

For more information:
Kids Are Authors® 1080 Greenwood Blvd., Lake Mary, FL 32746
Or visit our web site at: www.scholastic.com/kidsareauthors

ISBN-978-0-545-51574-0
12 11 10 9 8 7 6 5 4 3 2 1

Cover design by Bill Henderson
Printed and bound in the U.S.A.
First Printing, July 2012